A SOFT GIRL GONE ROGUE

Reclaiming Power, Peace, and Purpose

By Sheniqua Chantel Roper

Table of Content

Introduction

This book is not just a collection of stories—it's a sacred journey. A return to self. A reclamation of power, peace, and purpose.

These pages are born from real tears, real healing, and real awakening.

What you hold in your hands is part memoir, part mirror. My journey may not be yours exactly, but I hope you find yourself in the reflections, in the rituals, in the soft truths that unfold here.

This book is for the woman who stayed too long, doubted her worth, or silenced her voice. It's for the woman who broke the cycle, learned the lesson, and rose anyway. Wherever you are on your path—I see you. And I honor you.

Dedication

To my daughter—may you always know your worth before the world ever tries to define it for you. To my past self—thank you for surviving. To the women who came before me—your strength is the foundation I now stand on. And to every woman reading this—this is for you.

How to Use This Book

Move through these pages with intention. Let your intuition guide you. Each chapter ends with Reflections & Rituals—a sacred pause to process and integrate what you've read.

Use them in the way that best serves your journey. Sit with the journal prompts. Speak the affirmations aloud. Perform the rituals if you feel called.

You don't have to rush. This book will meet you where you are—and it will still be here when you circle back. This is your space to soften. To expand. To return to your truth.

Part I

Awakening & Alignment

"At times you gotta be real with yourself about the gap between the life you want to live and the life your daily habits are leading you towards."

—Anonymous

Chapter 1 – The Awakening

So there I was...

Sitting in my car behind a bush. On top of a hill. In the dark. Watching. Not because I wanted to, but because I needed to prove something—to myself. I was desperately trying to prove my gut wrong.

My intuition had been screaming at me, but I kept hoping I was just being paranoid. Shawn had told me he was working late. I wanted to believe him. We had plans. It was Halloween night, and I had carved out something rare: romantic, sacred time for just us. My daughter was at a playdate. I had made space—for him. But something in me felt off.

I texted to ask if he wanted food instead of me cooking. No answer. My stomach knotted. And when I passed the store near his job, the building was dark. His car was the only one there.

I told myself, "Maybe you're overreacting." But my intuition whispered back, "Girl, no you're not." So I waited. I sat in my car, behind a bush, on a hill like a damn undercover sister-in-law in a BET original. And then I saw it—a familiar car pulling up to his job. My heart dropped. Not because I was shocked—but because I wasn't.

It was her car. He got out the passenger side, moving like nothing was wrong, like he hadn't just lied to me about working late. That was all the confirmation I needed.

I pulled out, drove straight down the hill, and blocked their car right there in the middle of the damn road. The energy in my body was volcanic—hot, trembling, and loud.

I got out, stormed up to the car, knocked hard on the window, and looked him dead in the eye.

"What the fuck is this?"

He wouldn't open the door. So I opened it for him—and when I say I snapped, I mean I went off like spiritual warfare wrapped in a wig and edge control. All the lies. All the gaslighting. All the fake plans and sneaky links. Every single moment I ignored my gut to give him grace crashing down at once.

He got punched square in the face. The girl tried to pull me off him—she caught some too. It wasn't planned—it was a breaking point. A blackout. A holy purge.

My wig flew off. I didn't even flinch. I looked at her, calm in the chaos, and said:

"You can have him." And I meant it.

I was done with his broken, selfish, ego-driven ass. Done being his emotional air freshener while he left funk in my spirit. Done with his tired manipulation. Done with people mistaking my softness for stupidity.

That wasn't a meltdown. That was a rebirth in broad daylight. A few days had passed. I blocked him. I had called him so many times I lost count. Panic. Obsession. Desperation. Then I hit block and went ghost. It wasn't peace. It was emotional survival. But two days later, I unblocked him.

And the minute I did, he called me. I was getting ready for work, and this time? I was clear. He said, "I'm glad you answered. I just wanted to let you know I don't hate you. I care about you.

When you didn't answer, I figured you were giving me space." Sir... I blocked you. But I let him talk. Then I responded with grace and sharp truth.

I told him I was sorry for punching him—because I had evolved, not because I wasn't still furious. I told him I had finally seen the ways I was twisting myself to meet his expectations, while ignoring my own needs. I told him how he manipulated situations to keep me stuck, how he used my softness to validate his pain instead of healing it.

And I told him I was done. That I deserved better. That I would get better. That I wasn't her anymore. That wasn't a conversation. That was a final release.

After that, I went home and gathered every single one of his things. Packed them up. Dropped them on his driveway like I was cleansing my space. He kept calling. I didn't answer.

That week broke me. I tried to go back to work and act like nothing happened, but I wore my emotions like clothing. My therapist could see it before I spoke.

I requested two weeks off. Promised myself I wouldn't sit in the pain—I'd do the work. That's when I built my first healing routine: Meditation. Journaling. Eating clean. Exercise. Affirmations. Sleep. Grounding. Silence. By day four, I started to feel something shift.

I looked back at every time I ignored my intuition. Every time I silenced my inner voice— Sheniqua. Nikki. Niqua. Chantel. All of me, screaming under the weight of needing to be chosen.

I wasn't just heartbroken. I was spiritually malnourished. But the more I showed up for me, the more I started to believe: I am her.

Shawn wasn't love. He was a karmic trigger wrapped in good d and sweet talk. He wasn't the destination. He was the detour that led me back to myself.

My therapist once said, "Life is like monkey bars. You're scared to let go of one bar because you're not sure you'll reach the next. But what if you do?"

What if I fly?

I had to believe that I was worth the leap. And what I didn't realize then...was that this wasn't just about heartbreak.

This was spiritual warfare.

Reflections & Rituals - Chapter One

Affirmation:

"I will never abandon myself again. I trust my intuition. I honor my truth."

Journal Prompts:

- What patterns have I been repeating in love?
- When have I ignored my gut, and what did it cost me?
- What would it look like to choose me first, from this day forward?

Mini Ritual:

Write a letter of forgiveness to yourself. Apologize for the times you didn't listen, for the moments you settled, for the ways you silenced your voice. Then write a promise: what you will no longer accept, and what you're calling in instead.

Seal it in an envelope, light a candle, and say your affirmation aloud. You are now beginning again—with you.

🕯 Soft Reflections 🕯

_____

_____

_____

_____

_____

_____

_____

_____

_____

_____

_____

_____

_____

_____

_____

_____

_____

🕯 Soft Reflections 🕯

"Every storm is not a test from God. Some storms are from the choices you made."

—Anonymous

Chapter 2 – Spiritual Warfare in Dating

"Every storm is not a test from God. Some storms are from the choices you made." —Anonymous after Shawn, I took seven full months to myself. No dating. No entertaining. Just me—healing, learning, and breathing into the version of myself that had been silenced for too long. That pause was sacred.

During that time, I started dating myself. Solo dates became my ritual: dressing up for me, eating out alone, taking myself to the beach, laughing in the mirror just because. I was discovering the joy of my own company.

I promised myself I'd show up for me the way I always showed up for others. A few months in, I finally went to the Taste of St. Croix—something I'd always said I'd do. I even hit the after party at the Purple Lounge in Christiansted. That's where I met Brandy.

Yes, Brandy was a woman. But the connection? Instant. Magnetic. Soul-clinging. We met on karaoke night, and her energy had me lit up from the inside. I don't know what it was, but I literally clung to her. We clicked hard, exchanged numbers, and the vibe took off from there.

We went out a few times, shared laughs, flirty moments, and passion. The physical connection was magnetic— intoxicating even—but it kept me in a cycle that didn't feed my soul. I mistook passion for purpose. Chemistry for compatibility. And every time our bodies met, I lost a little more of myself. Parts of her even reminded me of what I had just left. But after about two weeks, her effort turned to shit. She got distant. Cold. An asshole, honestly. But I still wanted her.

She left for L.A. that summer for her birthday, and when she came back, she was even more distant. I started to match her energy—quietly pulling back. She noticed.

About a month later, after I had already started matching her energy and going ghost, she popped up at my house unannounced—playing a Jagged Edge song out loud like she was in a 2000s R&B music video. I think it was 'Walked Outta Heaven' or something dramatic like that. She stood there with her arms open like she was ready for redemption. Said all the right things: "I want you, babe." "I want to start over." "Let me show you I can be the person you need." She always knew how to reel me back in—with soft kisses, old charm, and the sweet talk that used to feel like home. I fell for it. Again.

That night, I let myself fall into the rhythm of her familiar charm—the kisses, the old sweet talk, the illusion of starting over. I wanted to believe it could be different. That maybe this time, it would stick.

She told me to come over to her house later. Said she'd make it up to me. We were three months into this hot-and-cold, back-and-forth, confusing ass cycle. But I still showed up.

I got out of my car and walked to her door. I called her to let her know I was outside. She didn't answer. That's when I heard her on the phone. Laughing. Loud. Talking about someone else.

Calling people "options," like love was some kind of buffet. And then? I saw her peek through the window. Baby, I ran to my car like I was in a movie.

I sped off, texted her a piece of my mind, and blocked her before she could even open the door. I had been an option before—and I swore I'd never be one again.

There were others, too. Like Leon, who said he didn't want anything serious but started acting like we were exclusive—until I called him on it. And Andre, who turned out to be married, even though he swore he wasn't. I wasn't afraid to disconnect with anymore. I was finally comfortable calling people on their shit. I saw the red flags sooner. I left faster. I was learning.

And just when I thought I had learned to spot the signs early, the universe sent me a final test—wrapped in passion and potential. Then I met Morris.

This connection was different, but familiar in the worst ways. He was quick to talk about the future—planning dates, talking about trips, saying things like 'we should do this together' as if he meant them. But it felt hollow. Like he was auditioning for a role he knew he couldn't maintain.

His words were soft, but his follow-through was weak. The kind of man who knew how to script connection, but not sustain it. And it didn't take long before the red flags started peeking through.

I actually cut him off once after a month of talking and his energy turned inconsistent. But I reached back out two days later—something in me felt unfinished, like the lesson hadn't landed yet. He showed up with charm again. Not love bombing—but just enough attention and conversation to keep me curious. I wasn't fully in, but I wasn't fully out either.

When we talked again, he casually admitted that he preferred dating multiple people. I told him flat out: that kind of energetic chaos didn't work for me. My peace wasn't negotiable—because I had just spent months rebuilding it. I had poured into my healing, my self-trust, my routine, my wholeness. And I wasn't about to undo all of that for someone who didn't even know what they wanted. I had finally learned that protecting my peace is not just self-care—it's spiritual survival.

Then came the forgetfulness. He started forgetting conversations we'd just had. I'd open up about something personal, and days later he'd act like it never happened. It wasn't just inconsiderate—it felt like I was emotionally invisible.

The last straw came one Friday. He asked about my day, and I responded with warmth and detail. He read the message and disappeared. A week passed. He popped up like nothing happened.

That's when I responded—gracefully, but clearly. I stood on business. I told him, 'You don't get to disappear and reappear like nothing happened. Wherever you were, stay there—and tell the dead I said hello.' When he asked if I really meant that, I replied, 'You're a smart guy. Don't ask me stupid questions.'

He wasn't mean, but he was unavailable. His inconsistency had me questioning if I was asking too much. But I wasn't. I was asking for the basics: presence, reciprocity, and respect.

Presence matters more than promises. And if they can't be consistent with the little things, they're not ready for anything sacred. Energetic chaos is not compatibility. It just leaves you emotionally ungrounded. And I don't need to prove my worth to be chosen. I just need to know it and walk away when someone can't meet me there.

He wasn't the villain—but he wasn't my match. That saga was messy, confusing, and sometimes hopeful. But it was my final test. That pattern was old. But my response? That was new.

That's when I stepped into my soft era. The version of me who doesn't chase peace—because I am peace. Passion disguised itself as meaning. Attention pretended to be affection. There was thrill—but no stability.

He would say one thing and do another. Make plans then disappear. Call me all day one week, then barely respond the next. I'd see him post online but not reply to messages. It felt like emotional hopscotch—like I was being conditioned to chase crumbs. He told me I was special, but his actions never matched the words. He'd show just enough effort to keep me there, but never enough to build anything real. And deep down, I started to feel like I was being used to fill a void he refused to face in himself. I wasn't crazy. I was being pulled into instability disguised as romance.

Before I even touched a candle or journaled a single word, my body started telling me the truth. I felt heavy around him. Like something was gnawing at the back of my spirit. I couldn't sleep well. My mind was constantly busy—replaying conversation, overthinking tone shifts, feeling anxious in my own skin. I would be fine all day, and then the moment he texted or his name came up, I'd feel an internal shift—tightness, doubt, static in my chest.

He had this pattern of emotional push and pull. One minute, he'd pour attention into me. The next, he'd vanish or act detached. I never knew where I stood. I kept wondering if I was doing too much—or not enough. His energy felt addictive but empty, like it wanted to stay close just enough to feed off mine.

He disrupted my intuition. I couldn't hear myself clearly. The more I tried to find peace, the foggier I became. This pattern went on for weeks—small highs, long silences. I'd bring up how I felt and he'd deflect or act like I was too sensitive. I wasn't sensitive. I was spiritually suffocating. That's when I knew it wasn't just emotional—it was energetic. I needed answers.

I began doing energy work because I knew something was off. I lit a white candle for clarity. I journaled. I meditated. But every time I tried to center myself, it felt like his energy lingered in my space. I lit two candles— one for me, one for him—and asked God, my higher self, my ancestors, spirit guides and universe - my whole spirit team for clarity. Something just felt nasty and dark in my energy. Just completely off.

The first ritual revealed more than I expected. The practitioner looked at me and said, 'His energy is aggressive.' She watched the flame and added, 'His candle is jumping out of hand—like it's fighting something.' His candle danced erratically, spitting and jumping like it was trying to talk back. Mine burned slowly, but steadily, like it knew it had to hold space for truth. The second time I did it, it felt like his energy was reaching for mine. His candle leaned toward mine, flickering hard like it didn't want to die out.

But mine stood strong. A kind of energetic force field surrounded me. His flame tried to cross it— and fizzled out.

That ritual didn't just shift the energy—it unlocked something in me. I wasn't just tired of him. I was tired of abandoning myself. That's when I knew I was being protected from more than confusion. I was being protected from returning to a cycle.

A week later, he called me. I answered. Not because I wanted him back—but because I needed to confirm what I already knew: he was still vibrating in my field. But I was ready to remove him.

The conversation didn't offer closure. It offered confirmation. I told him he didn't just confuse me—he drained me. And that I was no longer available for emotionally reckless men hiding their pain behind passion.

Morris was a mirror to everything I hadn't fully healed. Not abusive—but spiritually exhausting. I kept trying to decode his energy, figure out what it meant, and search for signs. It felt karmic, but I kept calling it chemistry. The more I leaned in, the more unbalanced I became.

He wasn't my twin flame. He was a spiritual distraction—one I stayed in too long because the passion felt purposeful. But it wasn't. After Morris, I didn't just grieve the illusion—I transmuted it.

That connection cracked open a deeper version of me— one that had always been waiting to rise. I no longer confuse being wanted with being chosen. I no longer mistake attention for intention.

Morris wasn't closure. He was clarity. He was the last test. The final storm before I stepped fully into my healing era.

Reflections & Rituals – Chapter Two

Affirmation:

"My energy is sacred. I trust my body, my spirit, and my truth. I release all who cannot honor that."

Journal Prompts:

- When have I ignored energetic red flags in favor of emotional comfort?
- How does my body react when someone isn't aligned with me?
- What spiritual or energetic boundaries do I need to strengthen?

Mini Ritual:

Take a white candle and a glass of water. As you light the candle, say aloud:

"I call back all parts of myself that I have given away. I cut cords that no longer serve me. I am whole, protected, and free."

Let the candle burn while you journal. When you're done, dispose of the water outside to symbolically release any lingering ties.

🕯 Soft Reflections 🕯

_____

_____

_____

_____

_____

_____

_____

_____

_____

_____

_____

_____

_____

_____

_____

_____

_____

_____

_____

_____

Soft Reflections

"You can forgive some people without welcoming them back into your life. Apology accepted. Access denied."

—Anonymous

Chapter 3 – The Rise of My Dark Feminine

She didn't arrive softly. She came with fire on her tongue and a sword behind her smile.

My dark feminine didn't knock—she kicked the door down the moment I realized I was shrinking myself for the comfort of men who couldn't meet me where I stood.

She's not the version of me who pleads or explains. She doesn't perform softness for those who mishandle her.

She protects the parts of me I used to abandon. She is the voice that whispered, "You deserve more," when I was almost ready to settle for less. She's the one who finally said, "Enough."

What Is the Dark Feminine (To Me) The divine feminine isn't just light and love. She's also the shadows you once ran from.

My dark feminine is the version of me who became friends with the demons that used to taunt her—the fear, the silence, the pain, the rage. There was a time when those shadows punked me out of being me. I would crash out emotionally, lash out, or disappear into hermit mode.

But I've learned: the dark feminine isn't about becoming chaos—it's about knowing how to control it. To dance with your shadows without becoming them. To set fires only when necessary—and to know when to walk away instead.

Before, my dark feminine was wild, reckless, and unhealed. Now? She's balanced. Still fiery. Still powerful. But intentional. Before I even knew her name,

I felt her stirring during my final encounters with chaos disguised as chemistry.

After Morris, I didn't just walk away—I rose. Something in me cracked open, but it wasn't broken. It was power buried under years of people-pleasing, over-explaining, and shrinking to make others comfortable.

Morris wasn't just a person—he was the final mirror, the last karmic tie sent to show me where I still needed to choose myself. That ending didn't break me.

It initiated me. I started moving differently. My softness became a choice, not a currency. My silence became sacred, not submissive. My intuition became louder than my need to be liked.

And that woman? She doesn't chase. She doesn't beg. She doesn't fold for fragments of love. She sets the tone. She trusts the vibe. She honors the truth.

My dark feminine taught me that boundaries are spiritual. That protecting your peace is prayer. That choosing yourself is not selfish—it's sacred.

And when she finally took the wheel, I didn't feel angry. I felt free.

Reflections & Rituals – Chapter 3

Affirmation:

"I honor the fire within me. My softness is sacred, but it is no longer performative."

"I release what no longer serves and walk forward in power, in peace, and in full possession of my worth."

Journal Prompts:

- When did I first feel the stirrings of my dark feminine energy?
- What relationships or situations forced me to set boundaries I used to avoid? How do I embody both softness and strength in my everyday life now?
- What does power feel like in my body when it is rooted in truth?

Mini Ritual – Dark Feminine Invocation Candle Practice:

Light a deep red or black candle. Place your hand over your heart and say:

- "I call upon the part of me that has been silenced.
- I honor the voice that protects, the energy that commands, and the love that does not beg.
- I reclaim the parts of me I was told to hide."

Sit with the flame for a few moments, breathing into your root and sacral chakras.

Visualize yourself standing in your full truth—bold, grounded, and radiant. When ready, write a short letter to your dark feminine, thanking her for arriving. Burn the letter in a safe fireproof dish, and scatter the ashes outside as an offering of transformation.

🕯 Soft Reflections 🕯

_____
_____
_____
_____
_____
_____
_____
_____
_____
_____
_____
_____
_____
_____
_____
_____

🕯 Soft Reflections 🕯

_____

_____

_____

_____

_____

_____

_____

_____

_____

_____

_____

_____

_____

_____

_____

_____

Part II

Love, Boundaries & Self Respect

"Stay away from people that still see the old you and don't respect the current you."

—Anonymous

Chapter 4 – Love, Intention, & Sacred Standards

After reclaiming my energy and standing fully in my power, I realized something else had shifted—my **definition of love.**

There was a time when I thought love was supposed to sweep me off my feet— fast, loud, magnetic. I chased the feeling more than the foundation.

But healing teaches you how to slow down. How to listen inward before leaning outward. How to choose love, not just fall into it.

This chapter isn't about blaming old versions of me. It's about honoring her, then choosing differently.

Because now, I don't just want love. I want love with intention. I'm standing on business when it comes to my heart—because peace, alignment, and reciprocity are the bare minimum.

A Poetic Interlude – What Love Is No Longer Allowed To Be

Love is no longer allowed to be:

- A game of guessing who I am to you.
- Loud apologies followed by quiet neglect.
- A place where I overextend while you under deliver.
- Passion that leaves me in pieces.
- Silence that feels like punishment.
- Half-effort intimacy dressed up as real connection.
- Emotional hide and seek.
- Another word for confusion.

Love must now be:

- Steady. Sacred. Sure.
- Aligned with my nervous system.
- Gentle in tone and bold in truth.
- A sanctuary, not a battleground.
- A partnership where softness is safe, not mistaken for weakness. I am no longer building temples in people who cannot hold divinity.

Reflections & Rituals – Chapter Four

Affirmation:

"I don't chase love—I attract alignment. My energy is sacred. I welcome only what nourishes me."

Journal Prompts:

- What did I once mistake for love that I now see as survival?

- What are my non-negotiable when it comes to love and partnership?
- How does my energy respond to emotionally safe people?

Mini Ritual – Calling in Aligned Love:

Light a rose-scented candle.

On a piece of paper, write the qualities you are calling in for your next aligned connection. Fold the paper three times and place it under the candle while you meditate.

Say aloud:

"I call in love that honors me, sees me, and grows with me. May it come in divine timing, in divine alignment, and in truth."

Let the candle burn safely while you hold the vision.

Keep the folded paper in a sacred place, or release it under a full moon when you're ready.

🕯 Soft Reflections 🕯

_____

_____

_____

_____

_____

_____

_____

_____

_____

_____

_____

_____

_____

_____

🕯 Soft Reflections 🕯

_____

_____

_____

_____

_____

_____

_____

_____

_____

_____

_____

_____

_____

_____

_____

_____

_____

"Every time you remember, forgive again."

—Anonymous

Chapter 5 – Letting Go & Moving Forward

There was a time when letting go felt like the end. Like failure. Like something slipping through my fingers that I should've tried harder to hold on to. I thought if I just loved better, proved harder, or stayed longer, maybe things would turn out differently.

But healing taught me something else: Letting go isn't giving up. It's coming home.

After reclaiming my energy, redefining love, and rising in my power, the next step wasn't finding someone else—it was finally releasing what I no longer needed to carry.

This chapter is about everything I released to reclaim myself. The people. The patterns. The pain. But more than that—it's about what I gained when I finally stopped holding on.

The Art of Letting Go

I've let go of lovers, but more than that, I've let go of survival habits that kept me in cycles. I've released the version of me who thought chaos was chemistry, who mistook attention for affection, who believed pain was the price of love.

I had to say goodbye to me who tolerated breadcrumbs and called it a feast.

The hardest part? Letting go of what was familiar. Because even pain can feel like home when you've lived in it long enough.

But peace... peace is unfamiliar at first. Stillness felt empty. Now, I know stillness is sacred. Silence doesn't mean something is wrong—it means I'm listening to myself.

My turning point came quietly. Not with a grand goodbye, but with a moment of clarity. A deep breath. A day when I didn't want to go back.

That was the day I stopped reaching for someone who kept proving they weren't reaching for me.

Release ≠ Failure

Letting go isn't losing.

- It's choosing.
- Choosing peace over potential.
- Choosing clarity over confusion.
- Choosing the version of me I'm becoming over the one I kept betraying to keep the peace.

There were days I spiraled, questioned if I gave up too soon, or if maybe I should've given one more chance.

But no. I didn't fail. I honored myself. I chose me. And that choice changed everything.

Making Peace with the Past

I no longer need closure in words. My peace is the closure.

I've stopped blaming myself for staying too long or loving too hard. That version of me wasn't foolish—she was hopeful. And I honor her now.

I forgive myself for the times I silenced my truth, for the ways I tried to prove my worth to those who couldn't see me.

I thank her—the past me—for surviving. She made it possible for me to become this woman.

The things that once shattered me? They no longer shake me. I can think of them now and feel... nothing.

Not bitterness. Not pain. Just peace.

Forward Looks Different Now

Letting go taught me that the unknown isn't something to fear— it's where all my becoming lives. It's where new alignment, new dreams, and a softer version of freedom began to unfold.

The future used to feel like a fantasy or a fairytale I had to earn. Now, it feels like something I am worthy of— right now, as I am.

My standards have evolved. I no longer dream of love that saves me— I dream of love that meets me.

Where there is alignment, effort, and emotional safety.

I'm no longer rushing. I'm no longer proving. I'm no longer chasing.

The new compass is clear: If it costs my peace, it's too expensive. If it confuses me more than it comforts me, it's not for me.

Living in Wholeness

I'm no longer seeking someone to complete me. I am whole.

Every goodbye I've ever had to say brought me closer to myself. Every closed door redirected me to a softer, more sacred path.

Letting go doesn't mean I'll never love again. It means I've cleared the space for a deeper love—one that mirrors how I now love myself.

I move forward with softness, with fire, with grace. Not because I've never been broken, but because I've finally learned how to hold all my pieces in both hands and say, "This is still enough. I am still enough."

And that? That is freedom

Reflections & Rituals – Chapter Five

Affirmation:

"I am whole without what I've released. I am worthy of the love and life I now create. I let go with grace, and I move forward with power."

Journal Prompts:

- What have I been holding on to out of comfort, not alignment?
- In what ways have I grown through letting go?
- What does freedom look and feel like for me now?

Mini Ritual – A Letter of Release: Write a letter to your past self. Thank her for surviving.

Forgive her for not knowing better. Celebrate her for all the ways she kept going.

Burn it safely, and as the smoke rises, say aloud:

"I honor the journey. I welcome what's next."

🕯 Soft Reflections 🕯

_____

_____

_____

_____

_____

_____

_____

_____

_____

_____

_____

_____

_____

_____

_____

_____

_____

_____

🕯 Soft Reflections 🕯

_____

_____

_____

_____

_____

_____

_____

_____

_____

_____

_____

_____

_____

_____

"You become your best self when you work on things people can't take away from you: mindset, character, integrity, authenticity, discipline, and kindness."

—Anonymous

Chapter 6 – Becoming Her

After learning to let go with grace, I finally made room to live in my fullness. Not as a version of me performing peace—but as the woman who chooses it daily.

There came a moment when I looked in the mirror and didn't just see the girl who had been through it— I saw the woman who made it through.

This chapter of my life isn't about proving I healed. It's about moving differently because I have.

Boundaries are no longer lines I explain—they're the air I breathe. Peace isn't a destination I chase—it's the place

I call home. I don't speak about my growth to convince others. I live it. I choose it. I return to it.

There's a softness in my mornings and a fire in my stride. I no longer seek validation in love or achievement. My existence is the proof.

I am her. Not in theory, but in practice. This is embodiment.

The New Me in Action

- **In dating**, I'm intentional. If the energy isn't mutual, I release without explanation. I no longer bend into versions of myself to be more palatable. I show up as I am—and if someone isn't aligned, I keep it moving with grace.

- **As a mother**, I am more present—not just physically, but spiritually. My daughter gets to witness a woman who values rest, who creates boundaries, who still plays, still loves deeply, but no longer overextends.

- **In friendships,** I stopped over giving. I no longer ignore how I feel for the sake of being liked or included. I trust my energy. I say no when I mean it. And I celebrate the ones who respect that.
- **At work,** I showed up differently. I trust my voice. I take up space without shrinking. I advocate for what matters. I don't wait to be given permission—I walk with authority now.

The Confidence Curve

There were moments I doubted myself. Old triggers whispered, "Are you sure?"

But now, instead of spiraling, I pause and ask, "Is this fear or intuition?"

Most times, it's just the residue of my past. And I honor it—without letting it lead.

The quietest part of me—my inner knowing—has become the loudest voice. I don't argue with my intuition anymore. I honor her. She never led me wrong.

Confidence, I've learned, isn't always loud. Sometimes, it's a calm decision in a stormy moment. It's the peace that follows a solid no.

Still Becoming

I'm not perfect. And I don't try to be. I'm not chasing healed anymore—I'm practicing wholeness in real time.

That means letting joy in. Letting grief move through. Giving myself grace when I misstep, and not over-apologizing for being human.

Healing wasn't a destination. It was a choice I kept making. And becoming her? That's an ongoing journey.

Some days I walk boldly. Some days I crawl.

But I keep becoming—with softness, with truth, with reverence.

Sacred Daily Living

Now, I start my mornings in stillness. A journal beside me. A glass of water on the altar. I speak affirmations over my day.

I light incense not to cleanse what's wrong—but to honor what is right. I walk slower. I eat with intention. I speak to my inner child often. I create joy instead of waiting for it.

Whether it's a solo date, a new lipstick, a playlist that sets the mood—I do these things not for show, but for soul.

Pleasure has returned. Peace is non-negotiable. I no longer perform healing. I live in it. This is me. Soft. Sacred. Whole.

Becoming her wasn't about becoming someone else. It was about returning to the woman I always was—before the world asked her to be small. And now...I don't chase becoming. I simply return to her—again and again.

Reflections & Rituals – Chapter Six

Affirmation:

"I am not performing wholeness—I am living in it. I trust my evolution. I honor my softness. I walk in my power."

Journal Prompts:

- How do I now embody the healed version of me?
- What choices or habits reflect the woman I am becoming?
- Where do I still need to offer myself more grace?
- What sacred daily rituals help me stay aligned?

Mini Ritual – Becoming Altar:

Create a "becoming altar."

Place one object that represents your past self, one for your present, and one for the version you are growing into. Light a candle in the center and speak over each one with gratitude, compassion, and intention. Say aloud:

"I am becoming—fully, freely, and in divine time."

🕯 Soft Reflections 🕯

_____

_____

_____

_____

_____

_____

_____

_____

_____

_____

_____

_____

_____

🕯 Soft Reflections 🕯

_____

_____

_____

_____

_____

_____

_____

_____

_____

_____

_____

_____

_____

_____

_____

_____

_____

_____

_____

_

Part III

Rebuilding from the Inside Out

"It's on you to get you where you want to be."

—Anonymous

Chapter 7 – Rebuilding My Life from the Inside Out

"Rebuilding from the inside out means choosing peace over pressure—again and again."

This wasn't just a reset—it was a renovation. From my finances to my focus, I rebuilt from the root.

There comes a moment in your healing when your outside life has no choice but to catch up with your inner evolution. When peace becomes too precious to trade for chaos. When survival is no longer the default—and you begin living with vision, clarity, and care.

I used to think healing was about feeling better. Now I know it's about building better. Better habits. Better boundaries. Better systems. Better self-belief.

This chapter isn't about perfection—it's about alignment. It's about learning to move through life not with panic, but with purpose. And most of all, it's about proving to myself that I could build a life that feels as good on the inside as it looks on the outside.

Healing Changed My Hustle

There came a point in my healing where it no longer made sense to live in survival mode. I had been hustling for years—grinding and burning out.

But the more I healed, the more I realized I was no longer driven by lack or fear. I didn't need to chase the bag with desperation. I had what I needed.

And from that place of gratitude, everything began to shift.

Healing gave me a new definition of success. It was no longer just about money or milestones—it was about alignment.

Peace became the new flex. Rest became revolutionary. Now, I move with purpose, not panic. I create because I want to, not because I feel like I have to. And that's where the magic lives.

Money, Worth & Energy

My relationship with money transformed once I stopped equating my worth with what I could earn or provide. I used to operate from a scarcity mindset, always worried about not having enough.

But healing taught me that abundance isn't about excess— it's about containment.

I began to see money as energy—something to flow with, not stress over.

I created two savings accounts: one for me and one for my daughter. Even if I could only start with $10 a week, it was a commitment to our future.

I started budgeting in a way that honored our needs and still left room for enjoyment. I downsized my apartment, limited unnecessary travel, and focused on essentials.

I even set a rule: We each deserve something once a month—because joy is a necessity, not a luxury. The biggest lesson? I learned not to delay investing in myself.

I used to talk myself out of ideas, only to look back years later and wish I had started. So I started.

I began laying the foundation for my YouTube channel—both for children's bedtime stories and spiritual content. I started this book. I put money into stocks.

And each step reminded me: Financial empowerment is a form of self-love.

Vision over Distraction

There were times when temptation knocked—an old flame, a new situationship, quick money schemes— but I started choosing my goals over temporary highs. I realized the importance of protecting my focus.

I didn't want to keep starting over. I didn't want to keep pouring energy into dead-end connections.

So I said no. No to men who couldn't match my energy. No to draining conversations. No to things that glittered but didn't grow me.

I chose peace over popularity. Legacy over lust.

Small Moves, Big Shifts I didn't wake up and suddenly have it all together. It was small moves—consistent choices.

- Saving
- Journaling
- Affirming
- Budgeting

- Creating calendar goals
- Decluttering
- Trusting the process

These weren't glamorous changes, but they were powerful.

Each decision helped me feel more grounded. More rooted. And slowly, my external world began to mirror my internal one.

I had systems. I had structure. I had vision. Self-Trust in Real Time.

One of the most profound changes has been how I make decisions. Before, I used to second-guess everything.

Now, I check in with myself. I listen.

If something doesn't feel aligned, I don't force it.

I trust my body. I trust my spirit. I trust my timeline.

Buying a home has become one of my deepest intentions. Not just for me, but for my daughter.

I'll be the first in my generation to purchase—not inherit—a home. That means something. It's emotional. It's spiritual. It's legacy. I've improved my credit. Built my savings. Picked up extra income streams.

I'm not racing anymore. I've slowed down, but I'm still moving—intentionally. Strategically. Faithfully. I no longer glorify being tired.

I no longer idolize hustle.

I believe in rest. In worth. In divine timing.

I'm rebuilding my life from the inside out. And this time? It's rooted in peace, not pressure.

A Quiet Confirmation

Recently, I received a message from a woman I barely knew. She told me that something I posted inspired her to finally start over. She didn't know my full story—but she felt my shift.

That moment reminded me: Even when no one's clapping, your alignment speaks. Your energy leads.

You never know who you're inspiring just by choosing yourself daily.

This is what it looks like to build sacred success.

Reflections & Rituals – Chapter Seven

Affirmation:

"I am building a life that honors my peace, reflects my worth, and supports my vision. I move with grace, clarity, and divine timing."

Journal Prompts:

- In what ways has my healing shifted how I approach money, work, or goals?
- What distractions have I successfully released— and how did it change my focus?
- What does a financially and spiritually aligned life look like for me now?

Mini Ritual –Abundance Intention Practice: Choose a quiet moment to sit with your journal or planner. Light a green candle (symbolizing abundance and grounded energy), and place a small object next to it that represents something you're building—maybe a key for a future home, a business card, or your child's photo.

Say aloud:

"I am rooted in clarity. I water what I want to grow. I trust the pace of my progress."

Spend time mapping one aligned action you can take this week—no matter how small. Let it be sacred. Let it be enough.

🕯 Soft Reflections 🕯

_____

_____

_____

_____

_____

_____

_____

_____

_____

_____

_____

_____

_____

_____

_____

🕯 Soft Reflections 🕯

_____
_____
_____
_____
_____
_____
_____
_____
_____
_____
_____
_____
_____
_____
_____
_____

"Your body doesn't just reject food; it also rejects energy. If your body starts rejecting certain places, people, or things, trust it and listen."

—Anonymous

Chapter 8 – Softness Reimagined

There's a softness that comes after the storm. Not the kind that breaks under pressure, but the kind that chooses stillness after learning how to survive chaos.

This softness isn't weakness. It's wisdom. It's the divine pause. The gentle "no." The sacred, self-honoring breath.

There was a time when I thought softness meant losing power—now I know softness is the power. This chapter is about reclaiming that power without apology.

What Softness Used to Mean

Softness used to be something I offered without question. It meant being the "understanding" one. The one who held space for everyone—even when my own space was collapsing.

I used to confuse being soft with being silent. I thought shrinking was grace. I thought giving endlessly was love.

I wore people-pleasing like a second skin and apologized for taking up space.

Sometimes, my softness was survival. If I kept the peace, maybe I wouldn't be abandoned. If I made others comfortable, maybe I'd be chosen.

But that kind of softness wasn't softness at all—it was performance. Self-abandonment dressed in kindness.

Why I Hardened

I hardened because I had to. Too many heartbreaks, betrayals, and "almost" turned my tenderness into armor.

Dating experiences with men who mistook my vulnerability for weakness. Moments when I showed love and got ghosts in return. Having to be strong for my daughter, strong for myself, strong when no one else showed up.

There were nights I stayed up with my daughter asleep beside me, tears on my pillow, because I couldn't fall apart—not when someone needed me whole.

I was tired of being "the strong one," but life didn't give me a choice.

So I built walls and called them boundaries. I protected myself with sarcasm, logic, and emotional distance.

I moved in masculine energy because I didn't feel safe being soft. And in all that hardening...I lost the gentleness I craved.

The Feminine Reclamation

My softness came back slowly—through healing, rest, and remembering who I was before the world taught me to guard everything.

I began to realize that softness doesn't mean being passive. It means choosing peace over performance. It means emotional fluency, not fragility.

I started listening to the little girl inside me who never stopped hoping for a world where softness was safe. I found power in my stillness. Magic in my gentleness. Strength in not reacting.

My feminine energy became a sanctuary, not a sacrifice. It didn't mean I stopped being assertive—It meant I became more intentional. More rooted.

Softness is a decision now. One I make for me.

What Softness Looks Like Now

Softness now is morning silence with a cup of tea. Long showers with incense burning. Saying "no" with love and not needing to explain why. It's letting people support me without guilt. Crying when I need to. Laughing from my belly. Wearing my silk robe just because. Letting myself receive, rest, restore.

Like the day I cried in the car and didn't rush to wipe my tears. I let myself feel. I didn't call a friend to explain or distract myself—I just held me. That moment wasn't dramatic, but it was sacred. I chose me.

I no longer feel like I have to be the strong one 24/7. I trust that I can be held, too.

I mother myself now. I speak gently to my body. I give myself grace when I fall short. I no longer chase love—I open space for it.

It took practice. At first, I didn't even know how to rest without guilt. My nervous system didn't trust ease—but I kept showing up until it did.

Protecting the Soft Woman Within

I don't offer softness to just anyone anymore. It's sacred. You have to earn access to her. Not everyone gets my tenderness, my emotional generosity, or my nurturing spirit.

Those are gifts, not guarantees.

Boundaries keep me soft. Discernment keeps me safe. And peace? Peace is my non-negotiable. I used to over-explain, over-give, and over-stay. Now I honor when it's time to leave.

Now I know: Protecting my energy is protecting my softness.

This softness? It isn't a return to weakness. It's a return to truth—the kind my body always knew.

Reflections & Rituals – Chapter Eight

Affirmation:

"My softness is sacred. I honor it. I protect it. I share it with care. I no longer abandon my peace to prove my worth."

Journal Prompts:

- When have I confused softness with self-abandonment?
- In what moments did I feel I had to harden just to be heard or loved?
- What does it look like for me to feel safe, soft, and supported now?

Mini Ritual – Sacred Softness Cleansing:

Take a warm bath or long shower.

Light a soft-scented candle (rose, lavender, or sandalwood). As you wash your body, speak gently to yourself:

"I release the need to perform strength.

I reclaim the grace of being held.

I deserve softness—within me and around me."

Afterward, write yourself a short love note and place it somewhere visible for the week— on a mirror, in your journal, or beside your bed.

🕯 Soft Reflections 🕯

_____

_____

_____

_____

_____

_____

_____

_____

_____

_____

_____

_____

_____

_____

_____

🕯 Soft Reflections 🕯

_____

_____

_____

_____

_____

_____

_____

_____

_____

_____

_____

_____

_____

_____

_____

"You know yourself better than anyone else, yet you crumble at the words of someone who hasn't even lived a second of your life. Focus on your own voice—it's the only one that matters."

—Anonymous

Chapter 9 – I Am Her

I've learned that I can do anything I set my mind to. That trusting myself—really trusting, not just saying I do—is the most powerful love I've ever known.

I've learned that boundaries, held firmly and unapologetically, aren't walls— they're portals to peace.

I now know that saying "no" is divine. That giving myself the very things I longed for from others— companionship, attention, celebration, care—is not sad or selfish. It's sacred.

Falling in love with myself has been the most beautiful reunion.

Facing my demons wasn't a curse—it was liberation.

I'm not "too much," I'm powerful. And the parts they tried to control? They were just proof of what they saw in me before I could even see it in myself.

Now I know: Peace is more valuable than potential. Love should never cost you your voice. And healing is a return, not a race.

I'm No Longer Her

To my past self: Chill, baby girl. It's okay. You were doing your best inside a whirlwind. You thought survival meant shrinking. But I'm here now—and we're thriving.

I've shed people who didn't see me. Released the lies I told myself to feel safe.

I'm no longer the woman who begs to be chosen, who abandons herself to keep the peace. I'm no longer guided by fear or people-pleasing. I don't need validation to feel valuable. I trust myself. I respect my growth. I walk differently now—not from pain, but from power.

But I don't shame the old me—I honor her. She survived so I could thrive.

Living in Wholeness

I used to think becoming her meant arriving at some perfect version of myself.

Now I know—it's a daily return. A sacred remembering. Not arrival, but embodiment.

Peace feels like presence now. It's no longer the absence of problems— it's the presence of self.

I no longer rush healing. I live in it.

My daily life reflects my evolution: I'm grounded, discerning, and deeply aware of what I allow. I love with boundaries. I lead with integrity. I rest without guilt. I release what doesn't grow me.

Wholeness doesn't mean I never fall. It means I rise every time— wiser, softer, and more aligned.

I no longer tolerate the half-hearted. I no longer chase. I don't need to be completed. I am already whole.

To the Reader

To the woman still healing: Start small. Sit with your breath. Take a walk. Say an affirmation. Give yourself five minutes of grace. And then do it again tomorrow.

Healing isn't linear. It's a spiral.

Some days you'll cry over things you thought you released. Other days, you'll glow like nothing ever touched you.

All of it is valid. All of it is you.

No one's coming to save you—but your higher self is waiting on the other side of this. Trust her. She's wise. She's ready. And she loves you.

And you're not alone. Every time one of us chooses healing, we ripple that power into the collective.

To my daughter, my future self, and every woman reading this: You will break cycles. You will build new blueprints. You will become who you've always been.

One step is all it takes

Reflections & Rituals— Chapter Nine

"I am the version of me I once dreamed of becoming. I trust my voice, I honor my journey, and I live in full alignment."

Journal Prompts:

- What truth do I now embody that I used to doubt?
- In what ways am I showing up as my highest self each day?
- What does it look like to lead with softness and still hold power?

Mini Ritual: Self-Crowning Mirror Practice

Stand in front of a mirror with a candle lit beside you. Look into your own eyes. Say aloud:

"I see you. I honor you. I am her."

Place your hand on your heart and close your eyes. Visualize a crown of gold, flowers, or flame being placed on your head. Feel it settle—not as fantasy, but as a symbol of who you've become. Whisper:

"I no longer seek permission. I reign from within."

Take a deep breath, and step forward—into the life that's already yours. You don't need to earn your worth. You are the miracle.

A Love Letter to Myself

Love... it's so nice to see you again. It's been quite some time. I've truly missed you.

I love the person you are—how you stand on principle, on truth, on business, on justice. I love the way you take care of yourself, believe in yourself, and care for your soul so intentionally.

You, Sheniqua Chantel, are truly amazing. Anyone would be lucky to have you.

In this lifetime, you're doing the dang thing. You're super smart. Incredibly resourceful.

And thank you—thank you for seeking me out, for being gentle and calm with me as I grow closer to you. This? This connection? I couldn't have imagined it. Honestly, I didn't even know it was possible.

I love how tapped in you are. I love how you love on yourself.

Sheniqua, I'm so proud of you. Thank you for being open. Gentle. Caring. Loving—with yourself. You, my dear, deserve that. Keep being genuine. Keep your intentions pure. Stay close to the Divine— and please, stop trying to control everything.

Trust divine timing. We—your guides, your higher self, the divine—are here for you. We're here to guide you.

We are all so very proud of you. And we love you. Deeply.

You're fine, babe. Mistakes? They're just part of the journey. Delays and detours—not dead ends.

Keep going, Love. Trust yourself.

You got this, sweetie. And you always did

Closing Pages

Through the heaviness. Through the reflection. Through the remembering.

May you walk forward with a softer heart and a stronger spirit. May you forgive your past, protect your peace, and trust your path.

You don't have to become someone new—just remember who you already are. The healed you is not a fantasy. She's already within you.

And every step you take toward her... is sacred.

Sacred Resources

Books & Podcasts to Feed Your Spirit

Books

- The Body Keeps the Score – Bessel van der Kolk (trauma + nervous system)
- All About Love – bell hooks (rethinking love and relationships)
- The Mountain Is You – Brianna Wiest (healing & self-sabotage)
- Sacred Woman – Queen Afua (divine feminine practices)
- Vibrate Higher Daily – Lalah Delia (spiritual elevation)

Podcasts

- Therapy for Black Girls – mental wellness & emotional support

- The Mantras & Motivation Podcast – spiritual alignment & affirmations
- Balanced Black Girl – self-care, growth, and softness
- The Self-Love Fix – for reprogramming patterns and reclaiming power

Journal & Affirmation Practices

Daily Affirmations (start with 1–3 and build as you grow)

- I am safe to choose myself.
- I do not chase—I align.
- My energy is sacred. I protect it with grace.
- Peace is my baseline. Love will meet me there.
- I am no longer performing. I am living in truth.
  Journal Prompts to Return To:
- What does my energy need today?
- Where am I abandoning myself, and how can I come home?
- How do I feel in my body around people I love?

- What does my highest self-want me to know right now?
- What am I still holding onto that I'm ready to release?

Ritual Tips for Everyday Healing

- Light a white candle in the morning and speak your intention aloud
- Keep rose water or Florida Water nearby for energetic clearing
- Do an egg cleanse monthly to check your energy field
- Take a spiritual bath with sea salt, herbs (like rosemary or lavender), and a few drops of oil
- Make your bed with intention—speak love over your pillows
- Charge your journal under the moonlight
- Sit in silence and breathe—that alone is a ritual

You're Already the Magic

Every ritual, affirmation, and practice is a mirror— reflecting you back to you. You don't need to be perfect. You just need to be present. Your healing isn't behind or ahead... it's unfolding right on time. Return here anytime you need a reminder.

Chakra & Energy Guide

We are more than skin, bones, and emotion—we are energy. And within us are seven main chakras—energy centers that govern how we feel, love, speak, and move through the world. When we feel off—spiritually, emotionally, or even physically—it's often connected to these centers being blocked, unbalanced, or overactive. Here's a simple, sacred breakdown of what each chakra represents:

Root Chakra

Color: Red

Location: Base of the spine

Energy: Safety, survival, stability

When blocked: You may feel anxious, insecure, ungrounded when balanced: You feel safe, secure, and supported by life

Healing tip: Ground yourself—walk barefoot, eat root veggies, breathe deeply into your belly

Sacral Chakra

Color: Orange

Location: Lower abdomen (below the navel)

Energy: Creativity, pleasure, sensuality, emotional expression

When blocked: You may feel numb, disconnected, or overly dependent on others

When balanced: You're emotionally open, creative, and connected to joy

Healing tip: Dance, journal your feelings, tap into your inner artist, take a bath

Solar Plexus Chakra

Color: Yellow

Location: Upper abdomen (stomach area)

Energy: Confidence, willpower, self-worth When blocked: You may feel powerless, easily manipulated, or doubtful

When balanced: You feel empowered, decisive, and self-assured

Healing tip: Speak affirmations. Set boundaries. Reclaim your personal power.

Heart Chakra

Color: Green (or pink)

Location: Center of chest

Energy: Love, compassion, forgiveness

When blocked: You may feel guarded, resentful, or struggle with self-love

When balanced: You give and receive love with ease and empathy

Healing tip: Practice forgiveness rituals. Breathe into your chest. Let yourself feel.

Throat Chakra

Color: Blue Location: Throat

Energy: Truth, communication, self-expression

When blocked: You may struggle to speak your truth or feel unheard

When balanced: You speak clearly, with confidence and authenticity

Healing tip: Sing, speak affirmations aloud, and write yourself letters you never send

Third Eye Chakra

Color: Indigo

Location: Between the eyebrows

Energy: Intuition, insight, spiritual awareness

When blocked: You may feel mentally foggy or disconnected from your intuition

When balanced: You trust your inner knowing and feel guided

Healing tip: Meditate. Journal dreams. Trust your gut— it's not lying.

Crown Chakra

Color: Violet or white

Location: Top of the head

Energy: Connection to Spirit, divine wisdom, higher self

When blocked: You may feel disconnected, hopeless, or spiritually numb

When balanced: You feel aligned with your purpose and at peace with life

Healing tip: Pray. Meditate. Be still. Open to divine guidance.

Final Energy Reminder:

You don't have to memorize these. You don't have to "fix" anything. Just start listening. Your body, your spirit, your energy field—they're always speaking to you. The more you listen, the louder your healing becomes.

Affirmation Practices &

Journal Prompts

Below are a few of my favorite affirmations and journaling prompts to return to when you need grounding, clarity, or courage.

Affirmations:

- I am whole, even when healing.
- I trust my intuition more than opinions.
- My peace is not up for negotiation.
- I don't chase love—I attract alignment.
- I am the version of me I once dreamed of becoming.
- My boundaries are sacred, not selfish.
- I honor my softness and protect my energy.
- I am safe to start over at any moment.
- I release survival mode and return to divine flow.

- I am no longer performing—I am living in truth.
- I am allowed to evolve at my own pace. Becoming me is a journey, not a deadline.

Journal Prompts:

- What does love look like when I give it to myself first?
- What cycles am I being called to break?
- When do I feel most aligned with my power?
- What am I ready to release to protect my peace?
- How can I create more sacred space for joy in my life?
- Where in my life am I still shrinking, and why?
- What truth am I afraid to admit, but ready to face?
- What does the healed version of me say yes to?
- How do I want to feel, and what am I doing daily to support that?
- What would my life look like if I fully trusted my intuition?

Chakras Diagram

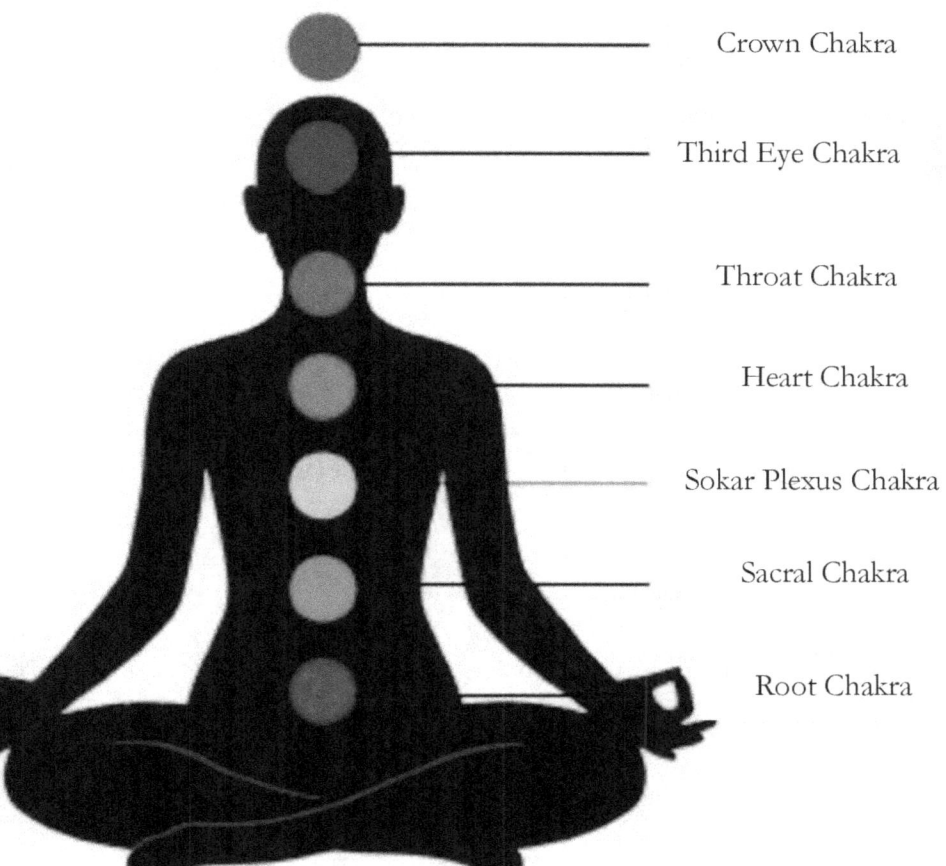

Crown Chakra

Third Eye Chakra

Throat Chakra

Heart Chakra

Sokar Plexus Chakra

Sacral Chakra

Root Chakra

Sample Healing Routine

This is a glimpse into the type of rhythm that helped support my personal transformation. Use this as inspiration—make it your own, adapt it to your life, and honor your energy each day.

Daily Healing Rhythm Morning Routine

8:00 – 8:30 AM: Meditation & Breathwork

8:30 – 9:00 AM: Gratitude Journaling

9:00–10:00 AM: Mindful Breakfast (without distractions)

Midday Nourishment

10:00 – 11:00 AM: Outdoor Walk or Nature Time

11:00 – 12:00 PM: Creative Play (writing, painting, hobbies)

12:00 – 1:00 PM: Intentional Lunch & Reflection

Afternoon Grounding

1:00 – 2:00 PM: Soul Reading (spiritual or healing literature)

2:00 – 3:00 PM: Journal + Self-Check-In

3:00 – 4:00 PM: Affirmations + Mirror Work

4:00 – 5:00 PM: Growth Work (podcasts, online course, wisdom notes)

Evening Wind-Down

5:00 – 6:00 PM: Self-Care Outdoors (sunset, barefoot grounding, movement)

6:00 – 7:00 PM: Set Intentions for Tomorrow

7:00 – 8:00 PM: Journal—What I Released, What I'm Grateful For

8:00 – 9:00 PM: Nourishing Dinner + Digital Detox

You don't need to follow this perfectly. Let it be a rhythm—not a rule. Healing isn't just about what you do; it's how you hold yourself through it.

Acknowledgements

To God, Spirit, my ancestors, and divine guides—thank you for walking with me. To my daughter, for being the light that brought me back to myself. To the people who broke me open—you were painful teachers, but necessary ones. To my therapist, my soul sisters, and every woman who ever poured into me when I couldn't pour into myself—thank you. To every woman reading this—I see you. I believe in you. This was written with you in mind.

About the Author

Author of healing. Vessel of truth. Woman becoming.

Sheniqua Chantel Roper is a storyteller, intuitive guide, and mother whose voice echoes the resilience, power, and softness of the divine feminine. Her work is rooted in spiritual healing, emotional reclamation, and the sacred journey of returning to self.

A proud daughter of the islands, Sheniqua uses her experiences with love, loss, motherhood, and personal rebirth to create empowering spaces for women to awaken, heal, and thrive. Her words speak to the woman who has stayed too long, doubted her worth, or silenced her voice—and invites her home.

This is her debut book. But certainly not her last.